World of Bugs
STRANGE SPIDERS

By Greg Roza

Gareth Stevens
Publishing

Please visit our Web site, www.garethstevens.com. For a free color catalog of all our high-quality books, call toll free 1-800-542-2595 or fax 1-877-542-2596.

Library of Congress Cataloging-in-Publication Data

Roza, Greg.
 Strange spiders / Greg Roza.
    p. cm. — (World of bugs)
 ISBN 978-1-4339-4612-7 (pbk.)
 ISBN 978-1-4339-4613-4 (6-pack)
 ISBN 978-1-4339-4611-0 (library binding)
 1. Spiders—Juvenile literature. I. Title.
 QL458.4.R69 2011
 595.4′4—dc22

                                        2010034393

First Edition

Published in 2011 by
Gareth Stevens Publishing
111 East 14th Street, Suite 349
New York, NY 10003

Editor: Greg Roza
Designer: Christopher Logan

Photo credits: Cover, pp. 1, 3, 5, 7, 15, 21, 23, 24 (eye, leg) Shutterstock.com; p. 11 Hemera/Thinkstock; pp. 9, 13, 19, 24 (eggs, web) iStockphoto/Thinkstock; p. 17 Robert F. Sisson/National Geographic/Getty Images.

Printed in the United States of America

CPSIA compliance information: Batch #CW11GS: For further information contact Gareth Stevens, New York, New York at 1-800-542-2595.

STRANGE SPIDERS

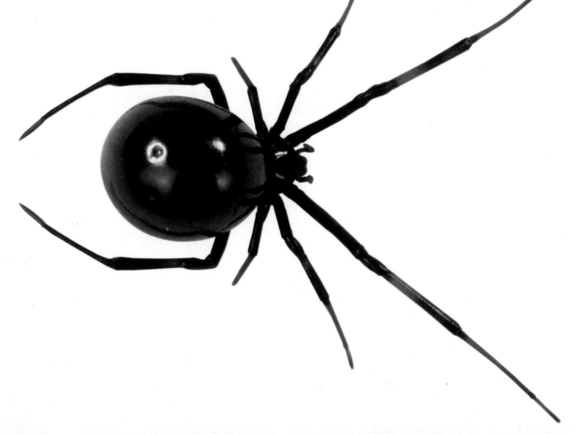

A spider has eight legs.

Most spiders have
eight eyes.

Most spiders cannot
see well.

Spiders make silk.

Spiders make webs.

13

Most spiders eat bugs.

15

The water spider eats fish!

Spiders lay many eggs.

19

Baby spiders come out of the eggs.

21

A wolf spider carries
her babies.

23

Words to Know

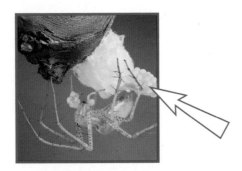

eggs

eye

leg

web